Orangutan

Children Book of Fun Facts & Amazing Photos on Animals in Nature - A Wonderful Orangutan Book for Kids aged 3-7

By

Ina Felix

Hello, I am Orange! I am an orangutan.

I am an ape.

I have red and orange hair.

I also have very long arms.

I use my arms to swing from branch to branch.

I use my arms to hug big and wide trees.

I live in the rain forest — far away from busy and noisy cities. But sometimes, you can find me in the zoo.

I make my nest high up in the trees.

Up in the trees, I see the sky. Up in the trees, I rest peacefully.

During the day, I eat. I travel from tree to tree looking for fresh fruits to eat.

I love to eat mangoes and figs. But most of all, I love to eat the fruit, durian!

Durians are spiky and smelly, but they are my favorite fruits.

When there are no fruits, I crack open nuts.

When there are no fruits, I eat leaves and insects.

When there are flies that bother me,

I swat them with branches.

When the sun is too hot,

I hide in the shade.

When the day is over and the night comes,

I climb up my nest and sleep.

I hope you had fun learning about my family.

Thank you.

Made in the USA
Lexington, KY
26 June 2017